Pig Coloring Book For Adults

Farm Animals Adult Coloring Book containing 40 Pig designs filled with intricate and stress relieving patterns.

Coloring Books For Adults: Vol 15

by The Coloring Book People

ISBN-13: 978-1543253696

ISBN-10: 1543253695

Preview Page

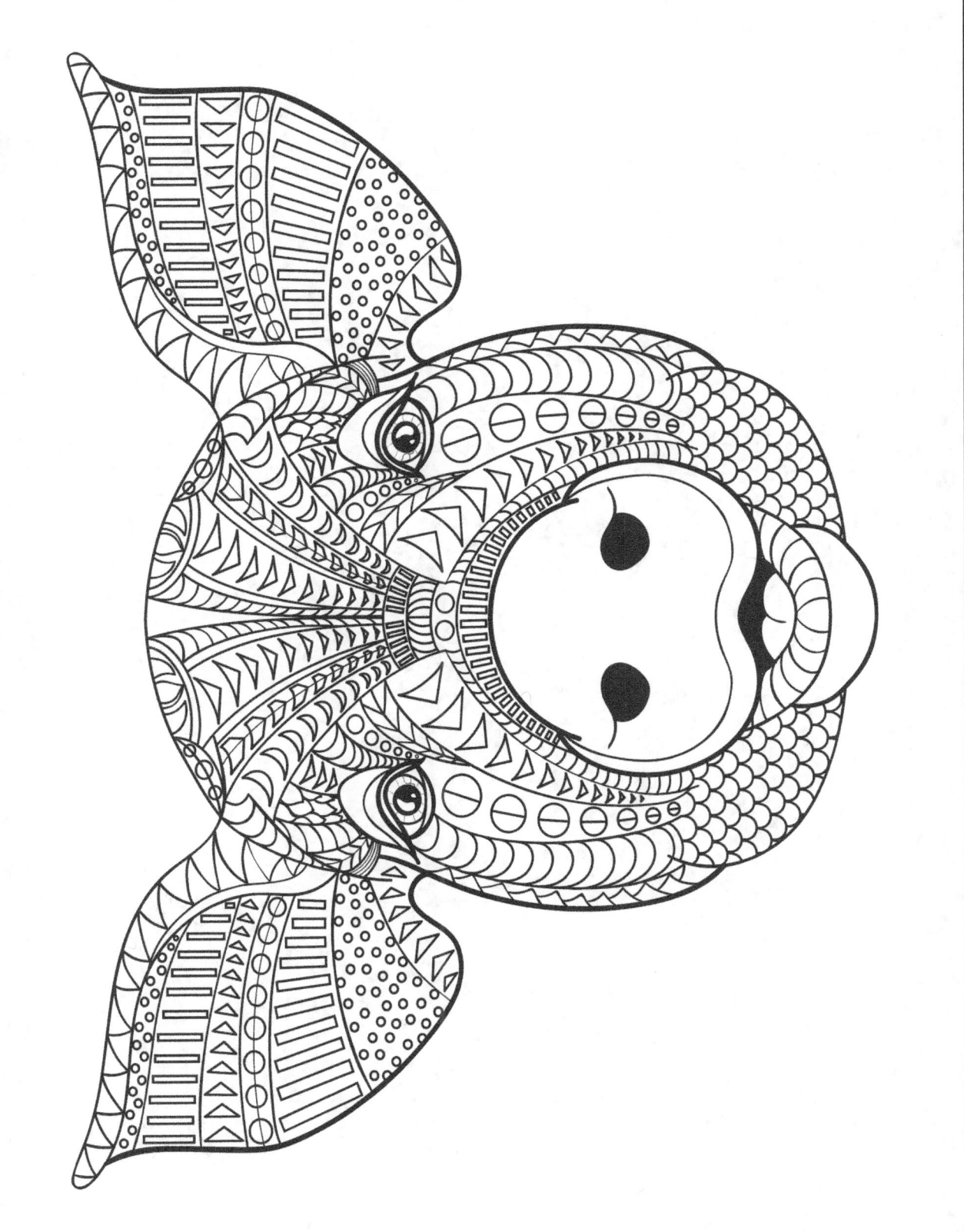

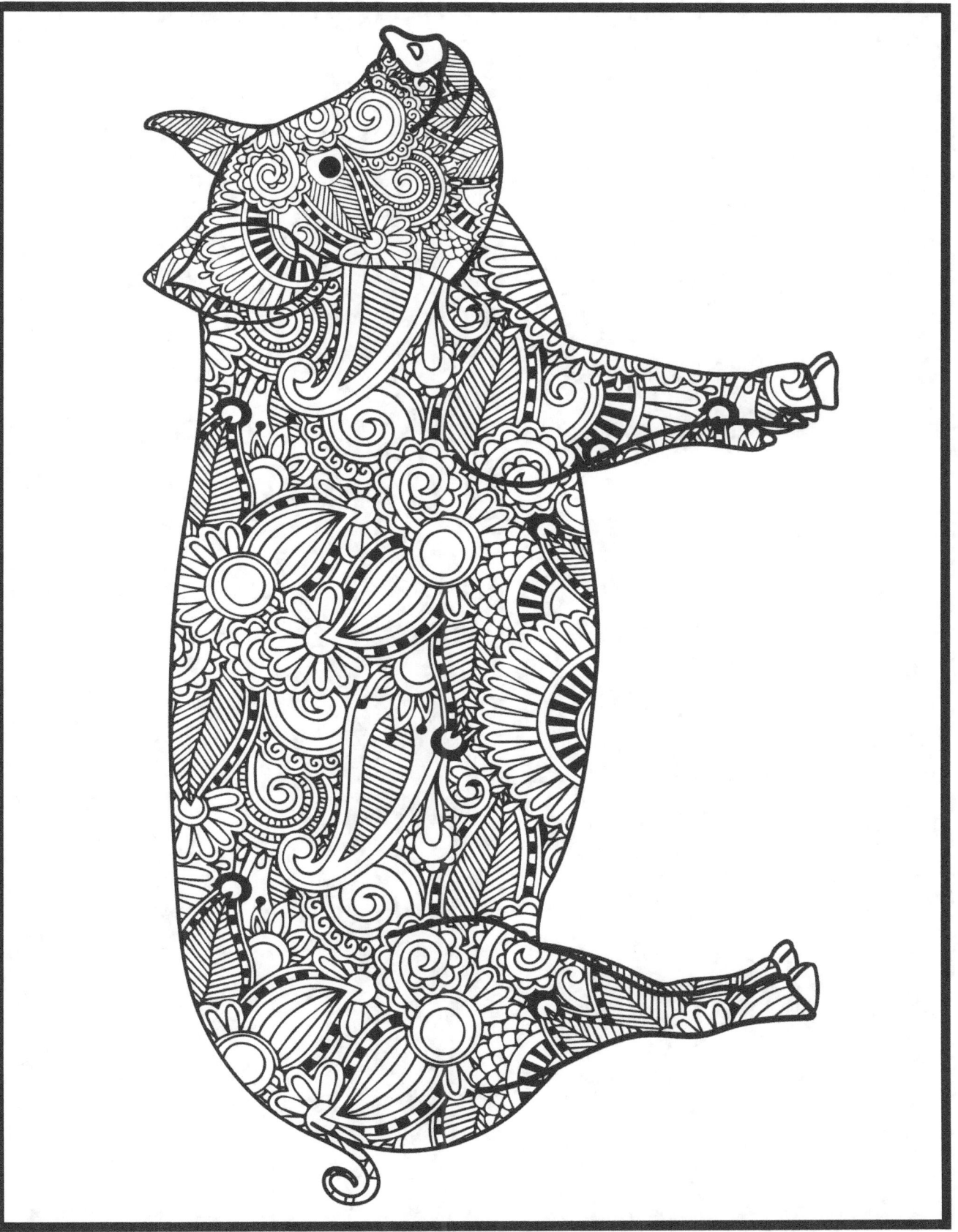

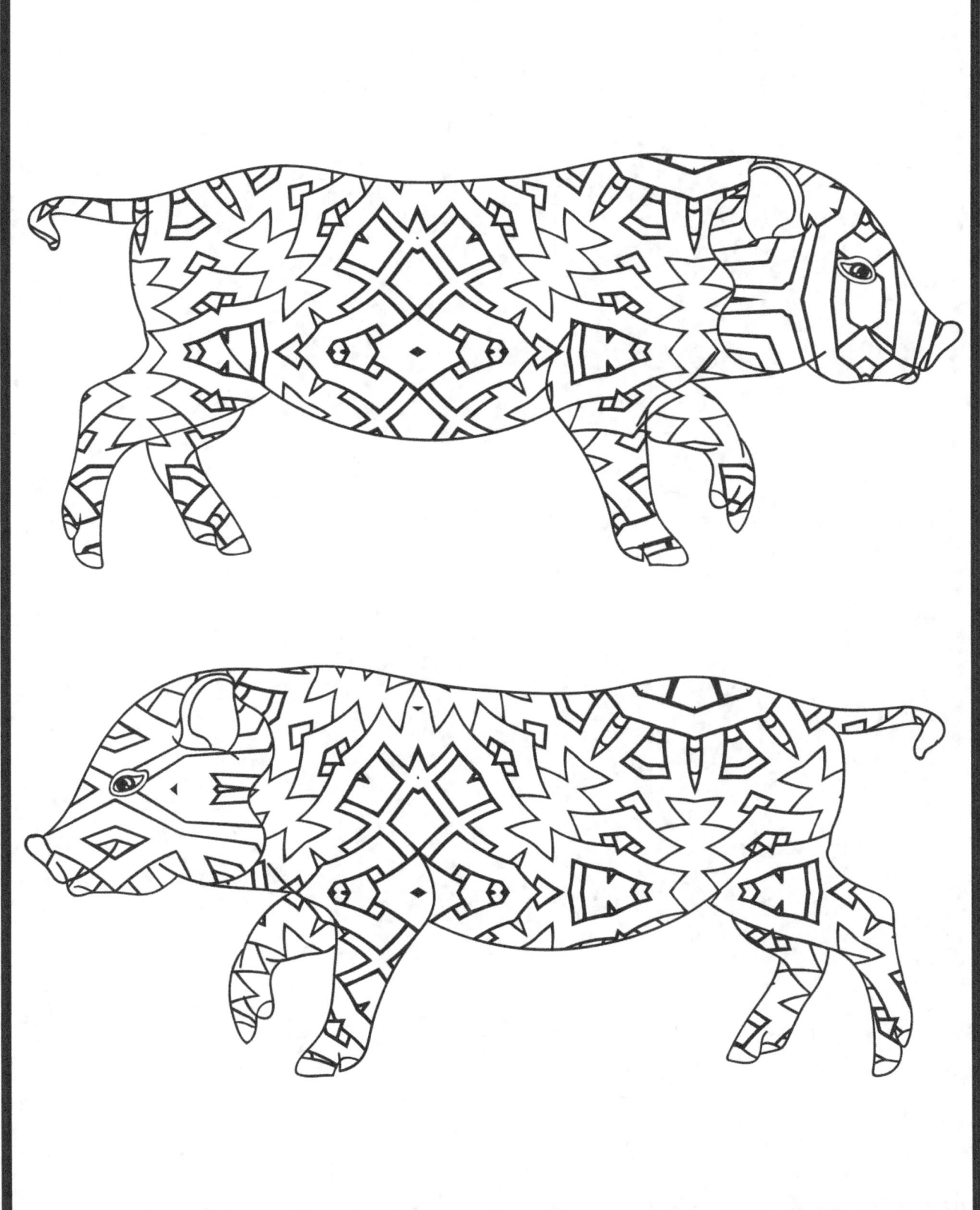

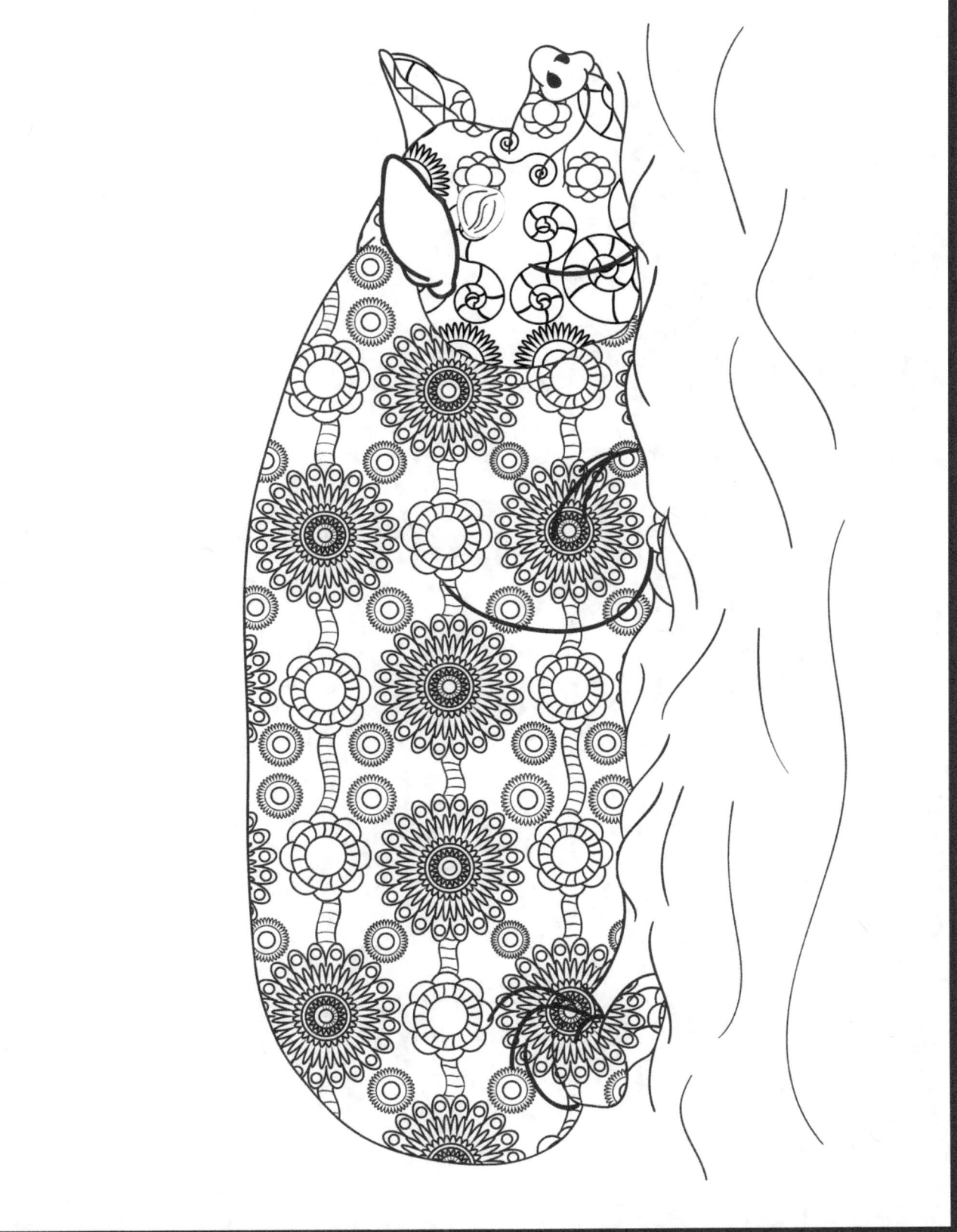

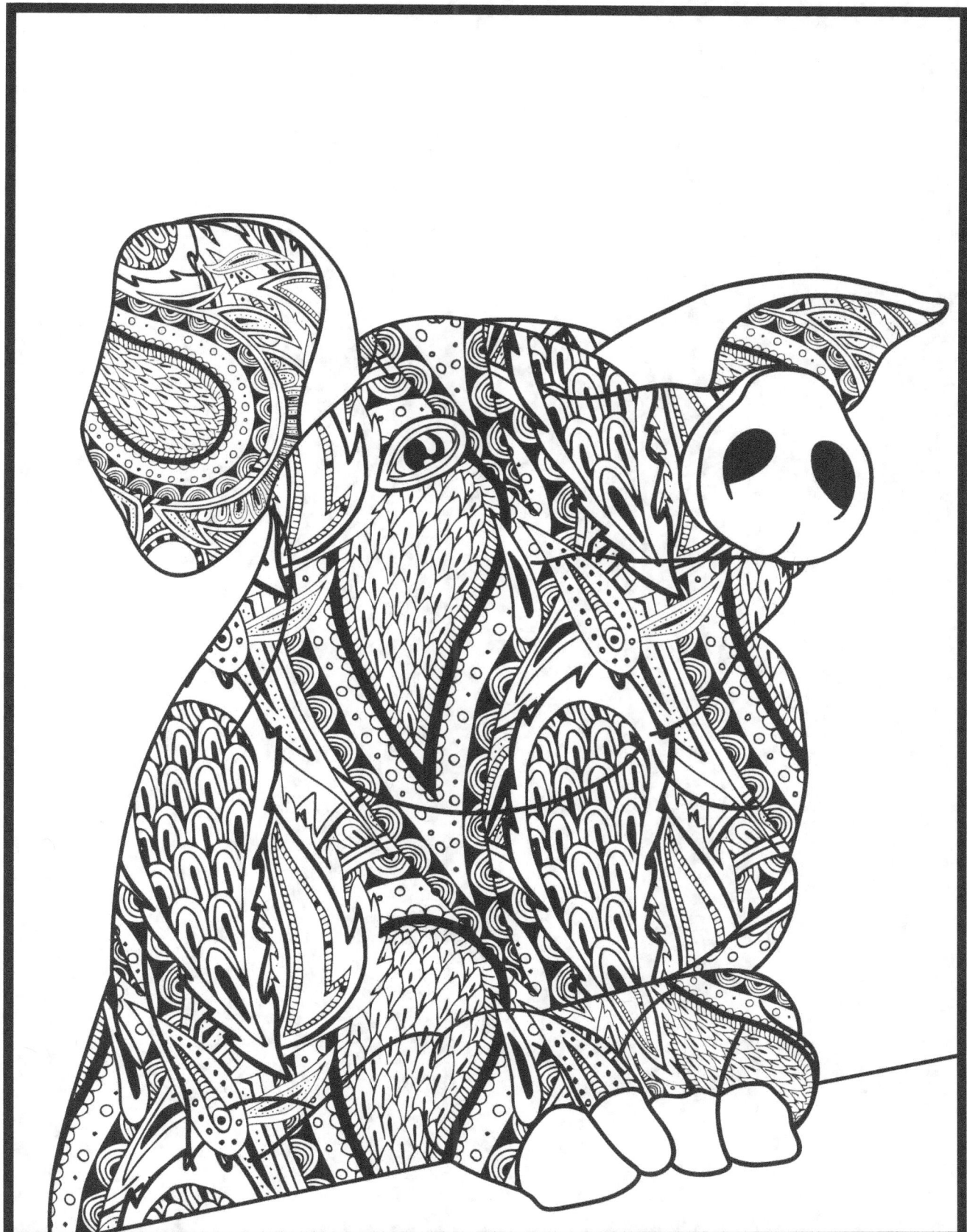

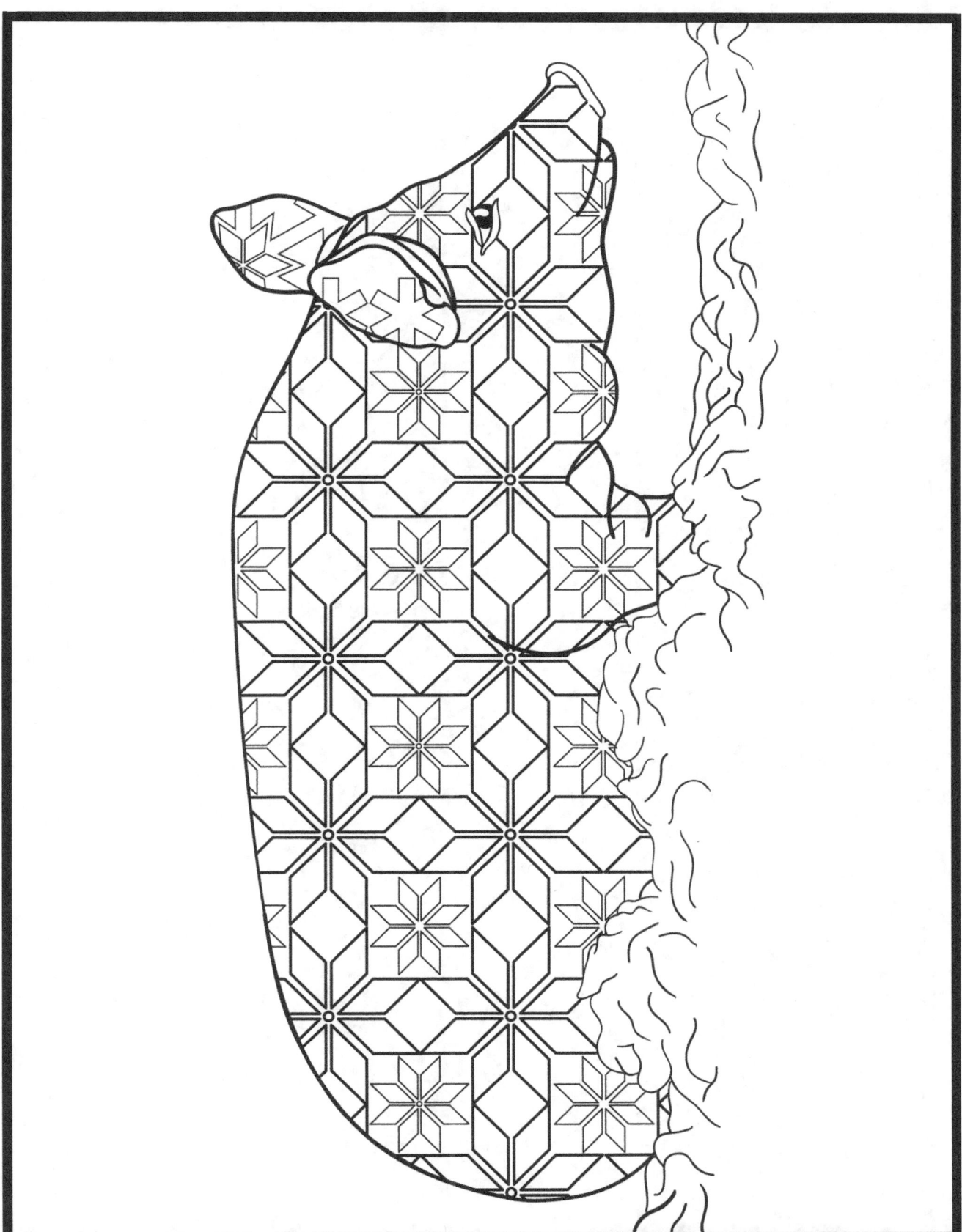

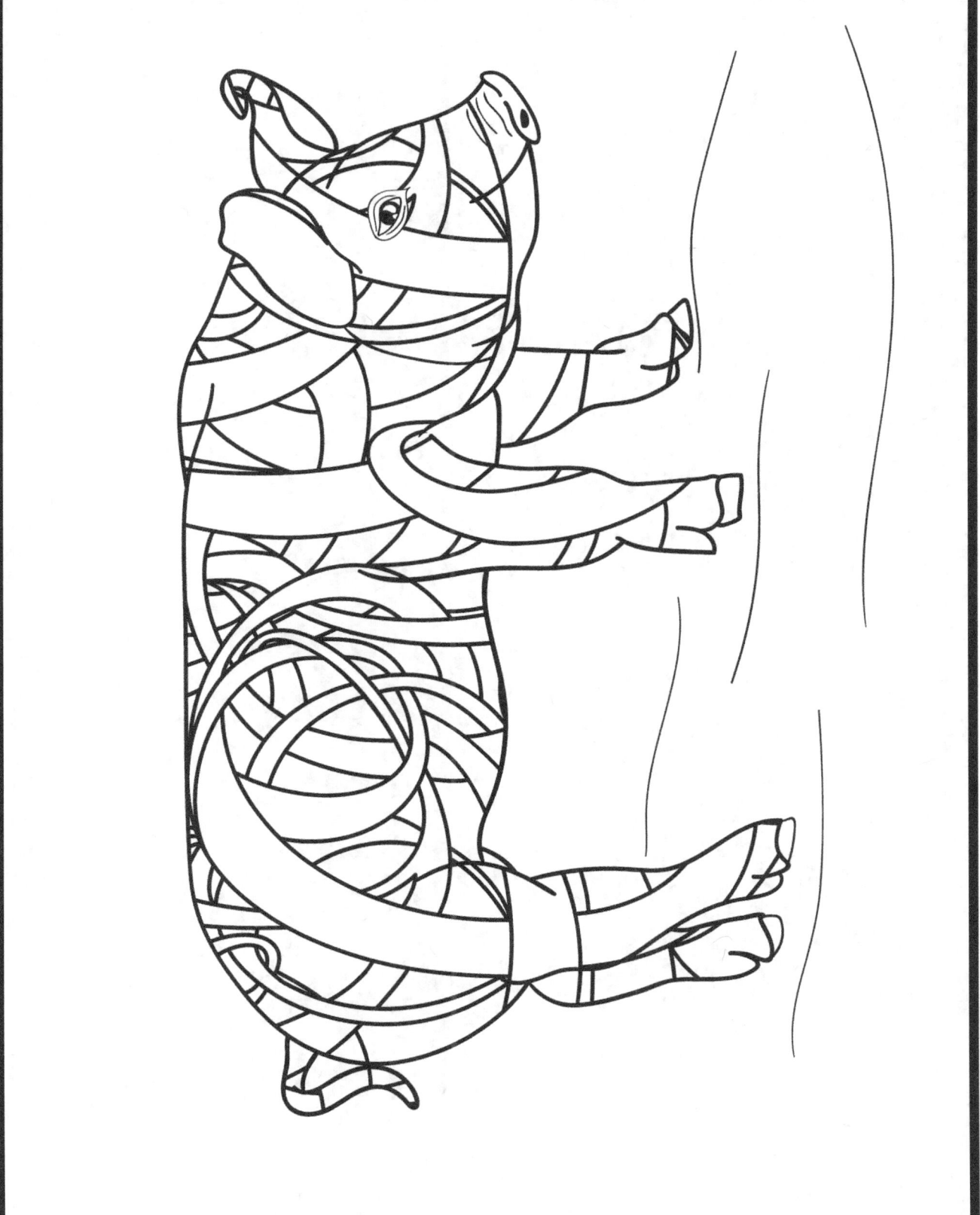

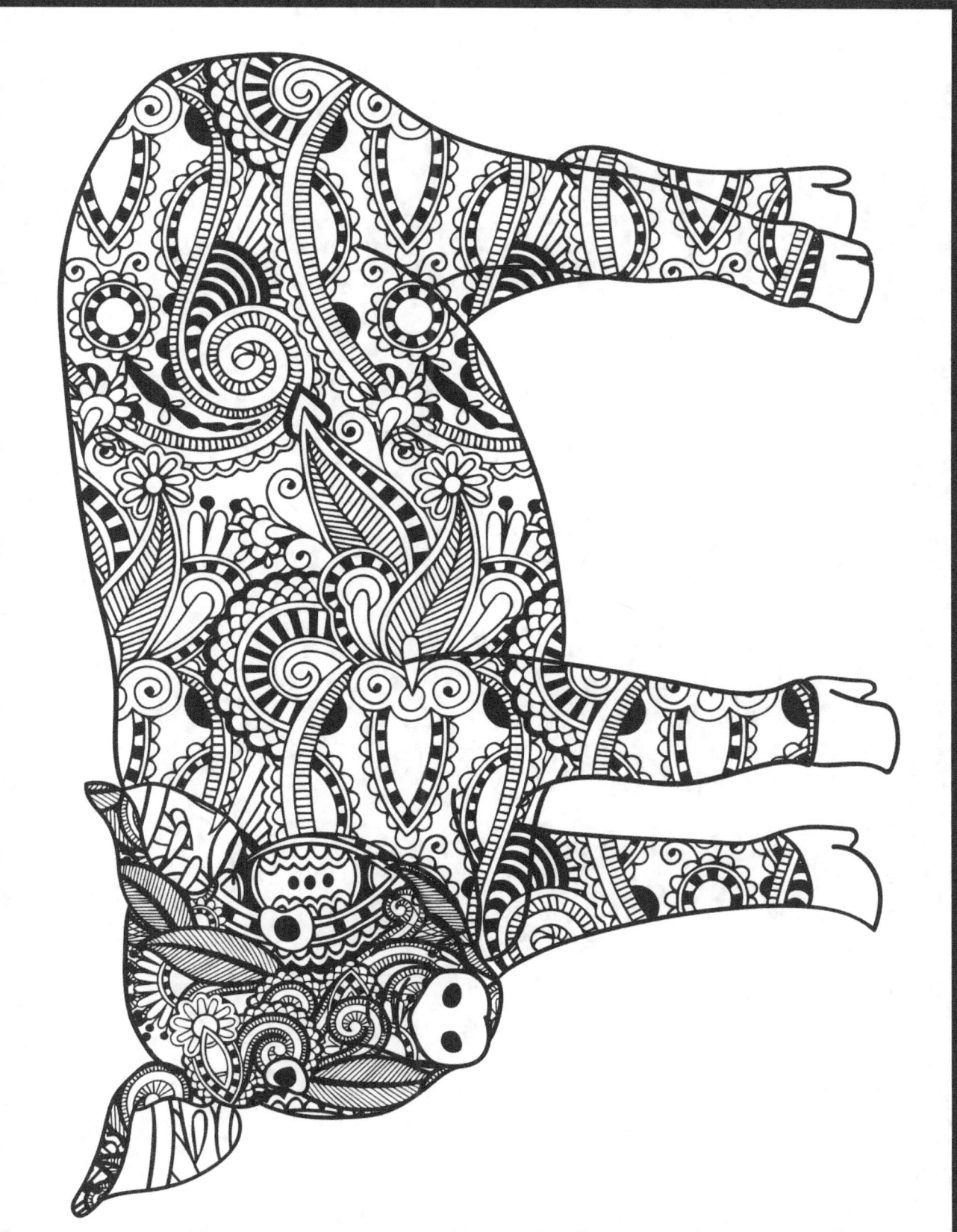

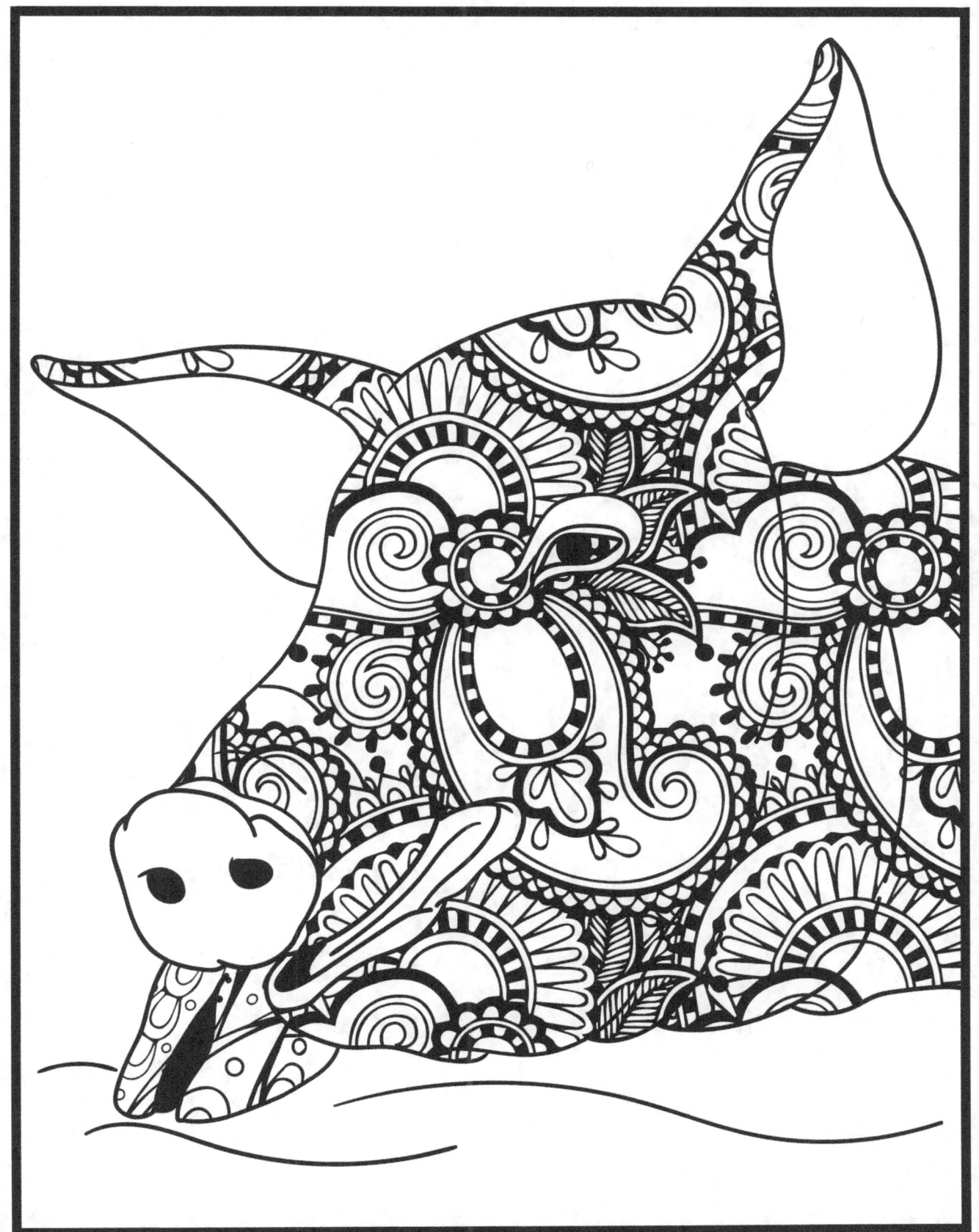

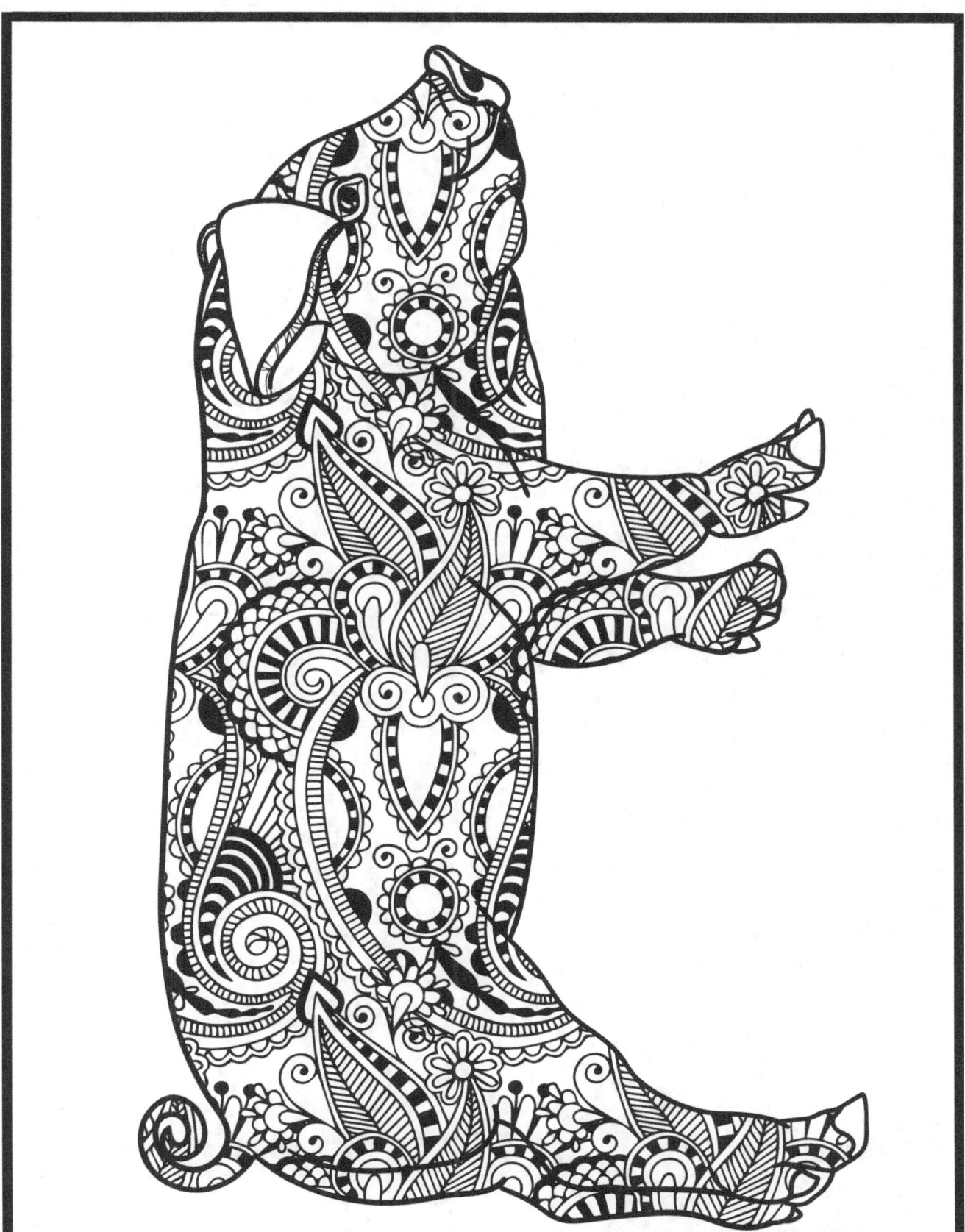

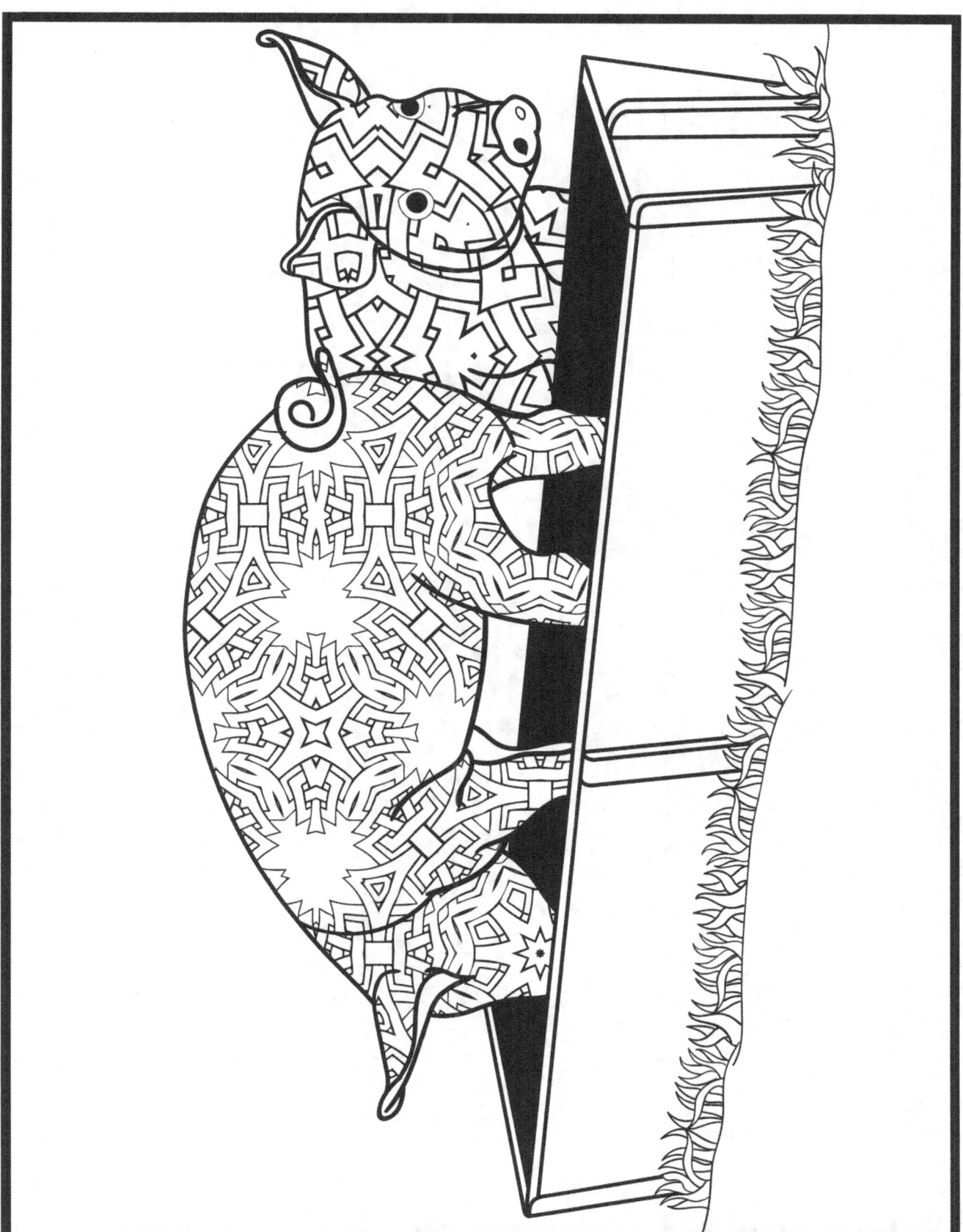

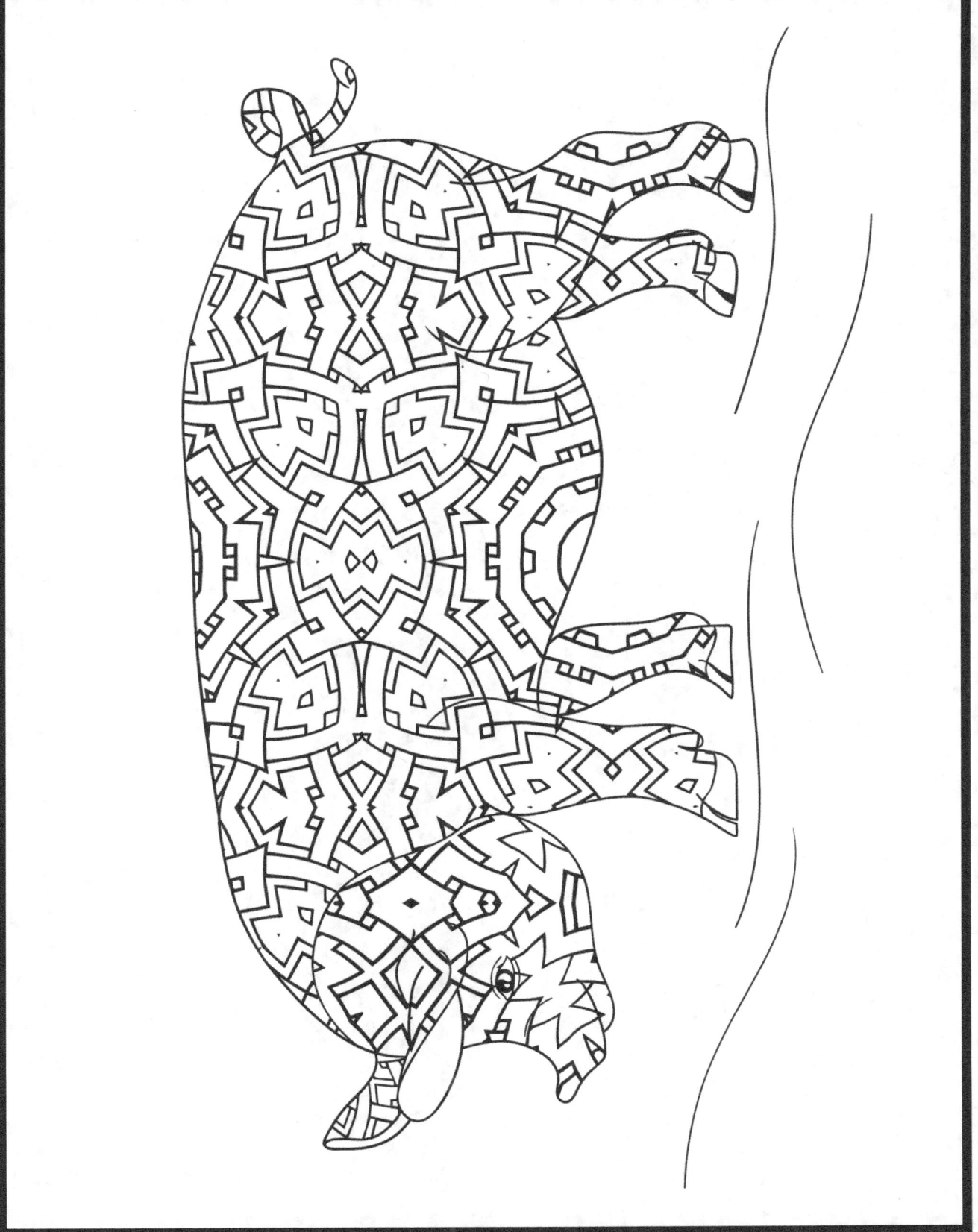

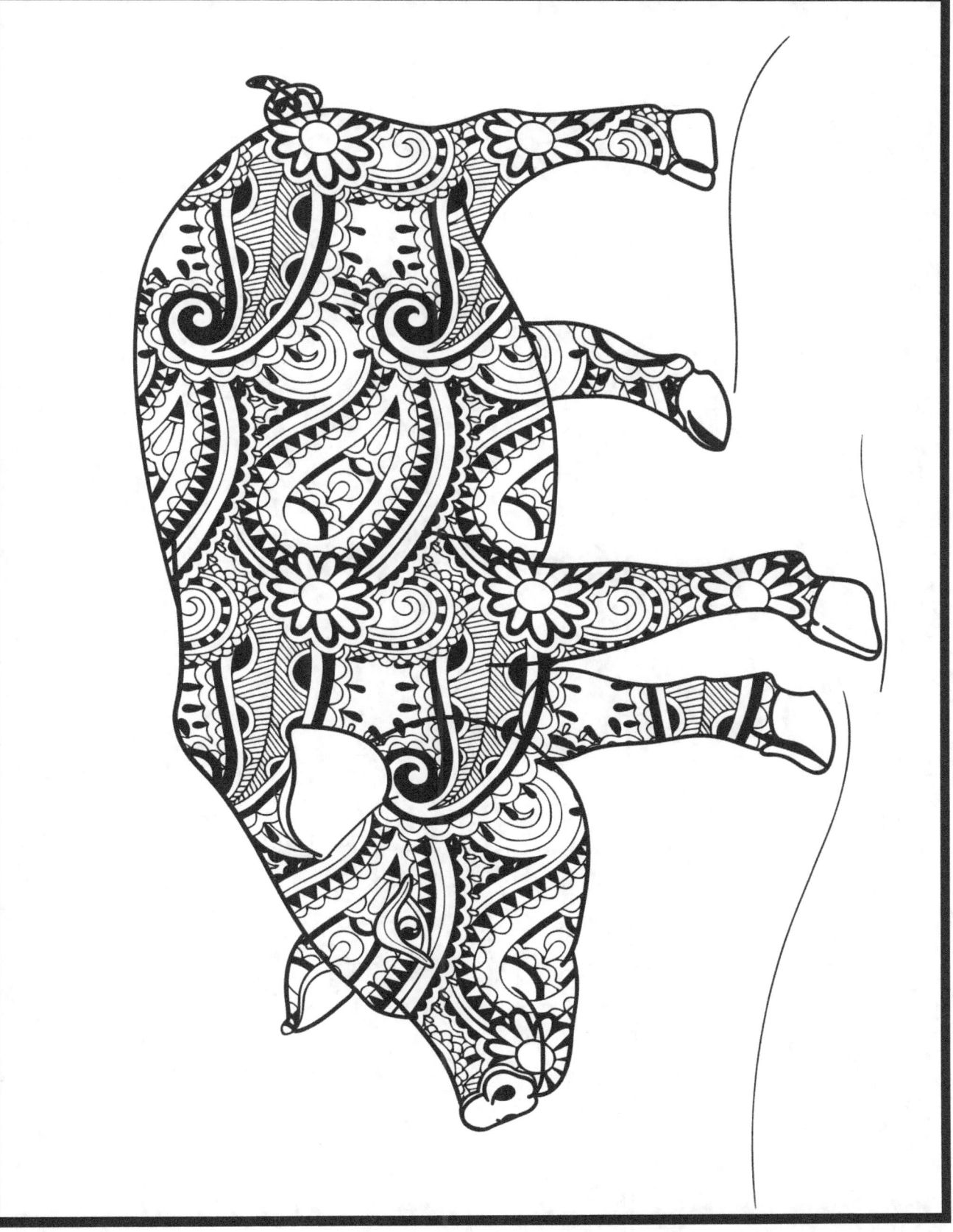

COLOR TEST PAGE

COLOR TEST PAGE